SII

Might And Inspiration

The Extraordinary Journey of Women's Existence

DIVYA PATEL

Business Woman | Social Worker

BLUEROSE PUBLISHERS
India | U.K.

Copyright © Divya Patel 2024

All rights reserved by author. No part of this publication may be reproduced, stored in a retrieval system or transmitted in any form or by any means, electronic, mechanical, photocopying, recording or otherwise, without the prior permission of the author. Although every precaution has been taken to verify the accuracy of the information contained herein, the publisher assumes no responsibility for any errors or omissions. No liability is assumed for damages that may result from the use of information contained within.

BlueRose Publishers takes no responsibility for any damages, losses, or liabilities that may arise from the use or misuse of the information, products, or services provided in this publication.

For permissions requests or inquiries regarding this publication, please contact:

BLUEROSE PUBLISHERS
www.BlueRoseONE.com
info@bluerosepublishers.com
+91 8882 898 898
+4407342408967

ISBN: 978-93-6452-160-4

Cover design: Shivam
Typesetting: Namrata Saini

First Edition: September 2024

Preface and Introduction

Just look at the whole world through my eyes,

Wherever you see, you will find,

Story of Sita, Savitri, Shakuntala is still going on,

See the world is watching the Queen of Jhansi

Create history today which talks about you,

The whole world resounds wow, wow, The Indian Woman

Truly this world is wonderful, beautiful. Everything is beautiful. And as this world progresses, much of its success can be attributed to the women of this world. Today, when the whole world is in a blind race to make women equal to men, when issues like women's rights are discussed globally, it is worth noting that India has been saying for centuries, since the dawn of human civilisation, that "यत्र नार्यस्तु पूज्यते रमन्ते तत्र देवताः।" (Yatra Naryastu Pujyate Ramante Tatra Devata.)

The meaning of which is that where women are respected, the gods reside. Woman is power. Woman is Amba (Goddess). Woman is the mother of the whole world. She is a symbol of love and emotions. A house does not mean four walls, but a woman's hands, a woman's heart that blooms in a house which makes a HOME. Let's listen to a conversation...

Woman: God, what makes you carefree?

God: Just you.

Woman: Hey Destiny, what is the secret of your happiness?

Destiny: That's all you are.

Woman: What's your best creation ever?

Destiny: Just you...

Thus Destiny also became free by creating a woman. And her best creation is indeed woman. She has many roles. A woman is a mother, a daughter, a sister, a wife, and a good friend too. She also becomes a Goddess when needed. She is Mahakali, Saraswati, and Lakshmi. And the same woman is also Jagdamba. Who has a flower in one hand and a weapon in the other. She also has a baby in one hand and a belt in the other... The woman is the idol of affection. She is a spring of love. She is Amrit. Woman is the incarnation of perfection.

Look at the history of the world; she has played all the roles when needed. And she excelled in all the roles. And that's why I feel like saying that...

On the earth, which is influenced by various flowers, you are best.

Poets begin to sing you as full of jewels, you are my mother, o earth.

This fragile, fragrant, scented of the universe is yours.

You are bravery personified, o woman, who brings out bravery from men.

When a woman becomes a mother... she has given birth to great warriors and great men to the world. Be it Mata Kunti or Mata Jijabai's Maharana Pratap or Jijabai's Shivaji Maharaj, Kaushalya's Sri Rama or Devaki's Lord Sri Krishna, Sita Mata's Luv-Kush. Be it Subhadra's Abhimanyu, Prahlada, or Nachiketa, Dhruva, or Anjani's son Hanuman.

When a woman has incarnated as a daughter... then she has also excelled in the world as great daughters.

Whether that daughter is Shakuntala of Kanva Rishi, or Sita of King Janak, Draupadi or Ahilyabai Holkar, or Maniben, daughter of Sardar Vallabhbhai Patel.

When a woman stands as a sister, she has done welfare of the world. In Saurashtra's village Una, the history of Aai Rambaima in Pinchhadi village in the name of Nandwana of Sri Maru Rajput Samaj is well known. There are many cases of sati behind a husband, but Aai Rambaima is exceptional in history in an instance of sati behind a brother.

When a woman incarnates as a wife, she becomes the embodiment of the world. And those names become tradition... Rukmini - wife of Sri Krishna, Sita - wife of Sri Rama, Draupadi - wife of Pandavas, Arundhati - wife of Vasishtha, Madalasa - wife of Ritudhvaja, Anasuya - wife of Atri, Savitri - wife of Satyavan, Girijabai - wife of Eknath, Rani of Jhansi, Ahilyabai Holkar, Ajabde - wife of Maharana, Rani Padmavati or Bhamati.

If you look at the history of India, you will understand that not once, but hundreds of Johars have been endeavoured to protect India, in which thousands of women gave their lives smiling. History is full of such examples, which illustrate the true importance of women. So I definitely feel like saying that,

We do not need Kohinoor, we are residents of Aryavarta, we birth live Kohinoor.

Somewhere in my country such living Kohinoor are still present.

Woman still shines somewhere here to keep the tradition of Mata Jijabai and Jeevatbai alive.

Hail to the women of Aryavarta

Who still incarnate Pratap-Prahlad-Shivaji somewhere. This is the history of great women of the world.

But today I want to talk about this book, named Sinha. But before that, let me introduce Divyaben. My native is Gir of Saurashtra. And Divyaben's hometown is South Gujarat. But only God knows who, when and how one meets in the journey of this life, but since my childhood, I certainly believe that not a single meeting in this life is the same. It also has the grace of God. That's how Divyaben and I were introduced. And Sejalben became the foundation link. Sejalben, who has a very good personality. She and I got to know each other through a group. After that, our acquaintance grew due to discussions of philosophy, religion and culture. Exactly during this time, I was introduced to her powerful team. All these my sisters have a definite place in my life now. All of them specially came to meet me at my house during the Tauktae storm. After that our acquaintance grew further. And then during the conversation, I came to know that Divyaben is very fond of writing. So often we used to discuss it too. Divyaben is a person who truly has a high emirate of heart. One cannot stay without realising her behaviour, her speech and her dignity just by meeting her. The way she has managed her home, her son and also a very nice home business/Grihudyog is an example for every woman.

Just before some time, we got to talking that she had been thinking of writing a book for a long time and she told me the whole subject of the book, which I liked very much. Its main subject was "a struggling woman who strives to be successful." And I liked the subject because it wasn't just about a book. It was not just a matter of language, but it was a story, a tale, a fact, an event... a document of the fact that goes on in every home. Divyaben's words have the beauty, simplicity, easiness of truth. The story of the heart of a woman has come out through Divyaben, who takes care of her own house. And I don't think house-keeping is a common thing, but they support their own household as well. Not only supports, but struggles tremendously. To become an ideal housewife who is not only Jagadamba/Goddess in her own home, but also Mahakali and Mahalakshmi in the world. Here we are talking about a woman who has thousands of questions while doing all this. When an ocean of problems surrounds you, how to solve them? This is its answer.

I had to give this saga a name that would do full justice to this entire subject. I read this book and saw a woman who fights, struggles. Achieves success by facing the questions. And sits on the pinnacle of achievements. Then I saw that such a roar could only be made by a woman with the spirit of a lioness, with the strength of a lioness inside her. As war is won, life is also a war. And a woman can play so many characters single-handedly, if she is not a woman who won a war and became great, not Bhavani, not Mahakali or the queen of Jhansi then who is she? Who herself has left for war. Riding on a horse. Holding a sword in one hand. Holding a shield in one hand. Wearing a saffron turban above, Jai Bhavani... went all out with the hail of Jai Bhavani. So doesn't she have husband, son or house? Alas, the matter is still incomplete. She has tied one of her sons behind her.. Aha... I am getting goosebumps just writing this. Salutes to this woman. I saw a lion in this woman, who is not afraid of anyone. Respects all, but not at the cost of self-respect. Thinking so, Sinha is named to this book.

Sinha, the name itself is awesome, means lioness...

It is not just a name. It's a reflection of entire history. Sinha is a saga that roars. Sinha represents the entire feminine world. We are not weak, but we have the power within us to build the world. The human beings whom the world bows to are born in our wombs. Be it the great Shivaji, Pratap or Prithviraj. Even if the creator of the world has to come as a human being, he has to come through us. Be it Rama or Krishna. Yes, I have different names. Sometimes I am known as Jijabai, sometimes I am known as Rani of Jhansi, but in the end I am a Lioness.

To all women of the whole world, I express my hope and faith to all of you that you also read this saga and your life will also become great in India.

Jai Hind.

Kumaril Rajput (Ahmedabad)

Date- 19/6/2024

|| Shri ||

Jay Mata Ji

यत्र नार्यस्तु पूज्यन्ते रमन्ते तत्र देवताः

Dedicated to...

If I were to write anything for myself, I would dedicate this book to my mother, Mrs Lataben Dilipbhai Patel.

Whoever I am today is because of her alone.

Obeisance to Lord Vedanarayana... Obeisance to Goddess Saraswati...

For this, I have received her blessings!

Introduction

I have been writing my "diary" since about 1996. Making the moments spent every day, my laughter, a pen and paper my friends, I open my heart and tell you my story.

This is my first book, and I salute my mother for making me worthy to achieve a high position in life. When I was young, I had a dream to become a writer, which will be fulfilled today with the help of my son Shivraj. I have been writing since childhood, but there was never a chance to publish a book.

I have graduated with a degree in History and Psychology. Currently, I am managing the Bhuwaneshwari Papad Gruh Udyog for the last 16 years, while also working with many social organisations.

The subject of this book is working women and office women.

In 2004-2005, I was a press reporter for the Bardoli weekly newspaper "Mega Gujarat" and also worked with "Bardoli Times".

1. The person who gave me the insight to start this book is also our Papad Udyog business mentor,

Gaurav Trivedi. He is a graduate in Information Technology and a Postgraduate in Human Resources Development. He achieved BULATS (Business Language Testing System) certification from Cambridge University at the age of 19. He has given more than 1,500 business training sessions.

2. At the end of each chapter, you will find correct advice and insight from those who have provided guidance:

Kumaril Rajput:

- Represents Indian culture, religion, and philosophy on various world platforms
- Participated in UNESCO's global competition for the best idea (Youth Citizen Entrepreneurship Competition) in 2018
- Represented India and Ahmedabad as India's first heritage city with Team UNESCO in December 2018

He has also given the name to this book.

Contents

1. Question 1
2. Struggle 5
3. Compromise 10
4. Adjustments 12
5. Simplicity 24
6. Success 32
7. Freedom 40
8. Women – Existence 52
9. Peace 63

1. Question

When in school, exams are stressful. We wonder when we'll grow up and be rid of this exam pressure. But as adults, we realise that life itself is a continuous exam, with no final result. Whether working women or housewives, one question has become common globally:

"What to cook this evening?"

I thought this question was unique to me, but I've heard it from many women. The reason I consider it a global phenomenon is an experience I had during a business meeting. It was around 4:30 pm when the phone of the man sitting opposite me rang. He laughed. Immediately after, the phone of the man next to him rang with the same question, "What to cook?" They both laughed together, realising that calls at this time are often about "What to cook?" I face the same question, but I've found a solution, which we'll explore in the next chapter.

This is a common concern for almost every woman. 80 to 90% of women likely face similar questions:

- I have to work from home because my family doesn't like me going out.

- I want to work and have the ability to earn, but my family says no. They tell me to stay home, eat freely, and take care of the house.
- I get a lot of work opportunities, but I struggle to balance them with housework and social activities.
- There are many jobs, but I don't have permission from home to work.
- The job is only for 2 hours, but who will tutor the children? The timing conflicts with their tuition.
- I can't pursue work I'm good at because everyone seems to dislike it.
- I'm told I can do whatever I want, but only after finishing the household chores.
- If I come home late from work, there's shouting and threats to stop working altogether.
- When I can't take leave from work, I'm asked why it wasn't difficult to take time off for the children earlier.
- Some say, "It's not our job to lift these bags. We can't provide door-to-door service." (This applies to beauty parlours, clothing businesses, or nail art work)
- If I don't attend family functions, relatives will be upset.

- Women also worry about potential sexual harassment or unfair treatment at work.
- Will I be able to leave work on time? Will there be overtime? Will I be paid on time?
- What about the office dress code (uniform)?
- My parents educated me well, but now they have to refuse my desire to work because my in-laws disapprove. We're all helpless.
- I've been and will be a daughter, sister, wife, mother, grandmother – everything. But what about me? What about my existence? Many women ponder this but often leave it unaddressed.
- The worry about what to make for dinner is real. What to pack in the children's lunchboxes in the morning?
- I must reach home by a certain time (2:30 pm or 4:00 pm) when the children return.
- I'm torn between family (home) and job. Which should I prioritise?
- I can't reach the office on time by rickshaw or bus. The commute is too long. I need a vehicle, but how can I bring this up at home?
- One question is the same for every woman: Going as a guest to her father's house and staying as a stranger in her own house. Who can answer this?

- I've taken too many leaves. Will I be fired? If not, will my salary be deducted?
- Where is the time for myself? It's said that God created woman with leisure, but did God forget to bring leisure into her life?
- After 40, when menopause sets in and my temperament becomes irritable and restless, will my family cope? Will they understand?
- I want to be something. I want to do something. My husband isn't cooperative.
- My business is slow at the moment. I'll have financial problems.
- I run a beauty parlour. My mother-in-law supports my untimely work hours, but when she goes for walks, there are discussions in the neighbourhood that affect my business.

Only those who have not been born to a woman, who don't have a sister at home or far away, who are firmly convinced that daughters will never be born in their home, can say anything disrespectful about someone's sister, someone's mother, or someone's daughter.

2. Struggle

A woman who struggles appears more beautiful than one beautified artificially.

I once heard a true story about the extent of a woman's struggle. It was set in a small Punjab village. A happy family arranged a marriage for their adult son with a beautiful bride from a distant village. After the wedding, she impressed everyone with her good qualities and household management. In time, she became pregnant.

Delighted with her life, she gave birth to a beautiful daughter. Gradually, the family's behaviour changed. She became pregnant again, delivering another daughter. The family's attitude worsened significantly, but she refused to accept defeat. After enduring her mother-in-law's taunts, she became pregnant a third time. When she softly announced the birth of another girl, chaos erupted. She was forcibly evicted with her newborn.

Weeping, she headed towards the railway station. In the pitch darkness, she stumbled into a room near a farm. Nature's curse or a mother's test, a violent thunderstorm began. Destitute, she wondered what to do with her daughter. She left the baby outside in the rain, which continued for three days. When the rain finally stopped, she expected to find her daughter dead, but miraculously, the child had survived hunger and the elements. The mother decided that if her daughter could overcome such natural calamities, she too could face her family's rejection. Her struggle was normal, and she would fight and survive.

This illustrates that a woman's struggle begins at childbirth and continues until death, yet she fights, wins, and lives on.

Working women face numerous challenges. Buses run late; rickshaws are expensive. Queues for bus passes are long. A 10-minute delay can disrupt the entire day. Women running businesses while managing families juggle multiple responsibilities, including their workers' livelihoods. The biggest question is what others will say when they leave home to work. This concern permeates their entire journey. When a mother-in-law questions her daughter-in-law's work, it reveals how women can be both enemies and friends to each other.

I recall a true story from a Women's Day celebration I attended as chief guest. A woman had single-handedly raised two successful sons through her tailoring work. Another woman faced a strict mother-in-law, a deaf and mute sister-in-law, and an alcoholic, gambling husband. Despite dire circumstances, she persevered, finding factory work and later learning beauty parlour skills. She managed household chores, raised two children, and worked door-to-door, all while enduring her mother-in-law's scolding and her husband's abuse. She even paid off her husband's drinking debts. One wonders about the limits of such tolerance, even for an independent woman. As her sons grew up, they became her shield against their father's violence. Though her husband remains an alcoholic, her sons' success offers some solace. Yet, what of her own future?

While writing this book, I've closely observed many women. Their primary fear stems from societal judgement and family honour. This fear is the chief guest in every woman's struggle, making her work not just challenging, but a true ordeal.

Consider a woman who treats her in-laws as her own, contributes to household expenses, loves her mother-in-law and father-in-law like parents, even sells her gold chain for household needs, only to be abandoned after five years when her husband finds another woman. Is this the predestined fate of women? Certainly not.

I interviewed several working women about their experiences. While they enjoyed their work, finding time for themselves proved difficult. The greatest challenge arises during menstruation when they must balance both work and home responsibilities. Unlike homemakers who can rest, working women must push through pain, discomfort, and heavy bleeding to fulfil their duties with a smile.

The struggle in my mother's life, to whom I dedicate this book, is beyond imagination. She would handle cow dung with one hand, clean animal waste, and transport 70 litres of milk to the village, all to ensure her children received a good education and life. This was 40 years ago, without modern conveniences. Even now, many villages lag decades behind in development.

I've witnessed a woman (my mother) protecting livestock during pitch-dark nights and thunderstorms, safeguarding their food, all while maintaining a sweet smile. Her simple desire: to care for these animals in her loneliness, as her son works in the city. What a struggle her life must have been, yet it remains unchanged today.

A working woman's daily routine is gruelling: preparing meals, managing household chores, caring for family members, commuting to work, shopping for groceries, helping children with homework, and supporting her husband – all while worrying about her own job responsibilities. It's rare to see men taking time off work for household duties, though post-COVID, about 25% of homes have seen increased male participation in domestic tasks. However, 75% of households still adhere to a male-dominated system, deeply ingrained in our social structure.

Society often questions women's choices. When my mother started her papad business 25 years ago, people questioned who would marry her beautiful daughters. She responded confidently, asserting that her daughters brought their own fortune and that she earned honestly through hard work.

Women's endurance is incredible, risking their lives to bring new life into the world. "The creation of woman on earth is the masterpiece of nature's work."

Today's "Gen Z" is more progressive, with young men more likely to participate in household work and support their wives while also caring for their parents. We must encourage this free thinking to avoid perpetuating conservative ideas that hinder personal growth.

A particularly hurtful phrase for working women is, "Now that you're earning, you've become more stubborn at home." I once overheard someone saying this to his wife. A woman fulfils everyone's desires at home, but often, people forget she has a heart too.

A woman's first love is her self-respect. Yet, she often compromises to keep the family together, even in the face of insults. We must raise a new generation to avoid such humiliation and conflict, instilling good values so that no one mocks our sons with the old proverb "henpecked husband".

मैं दर्द के आग को भी, फूलो की बाग़ बना दूं।
संघर्ष भले ज़ारी हो, मैं भी एक नारी हूं।

3. Compromise

As women, we've been raised to believe that household care is solely our responsibility. This mindset is deeply ingrained in both society and family, and we often accept this compromise. A woman's strength allows her to become a son when her father needs her and a father to her children when they require it, proving her worth in every role.

The first compromise a woman faces is adapting to a new environment after marriage—a different setting with unfamiliar people. Further compromises follow with each step up the ladder of life. A certain level of compromise is necessary and even expected. Why? Because it's what defines a wise and intelligent woman. She understands that her compromises keep two families united.

Without prior familiarity or experience, she must establish herself in her new home forever. Many films and stories have emerged to give women a breath of fresh air or to express suppressed emotions. 'Hellaro' depicts a drummer who unleashes women's repressed emotions through his beats. 'Kutch Express', a Gujarati film, shows village brides gathering after 11 pm in a backyard, calling it their 'whistle' or kitty party. They meet to alleviate the day's fatigue and share their deepest feelings. The film beautifully illustrates how this gathering becomes their only respite in life. Even if you haven't seen it, it's worth watching to understand the complexity of conflict resolution—whether to follow one's mind or heart.

Any problem must be solved, either through your own thoughts or with others' advice. Be cautious about who advises you, remembering that Duryodhana had Shakuni as his advisor, while Arjuna had Sri Krishna.

Compromise is necessary with time. You can solve 80% of your problems yourself, whether they're family or business-related. Even female CEOs of large companies face such questions. They move forward by reconciling with these issues, pondering over their confusion, and finding solutions.

Let's explore how to plan with compromise:

अगनपंथ की अदम्य, अभूतपूर्व, अविरत आग हूं मैं,
बारिशों को दिलमे रखा हुआ बेमिसाल बाग हूं मैं,।
नैराश्य से नूतन तक जाने वाला नगाधिराज नाग हूं मैं।
दर्द भरे कितने ही आँधियों को समाए रेशमी राग हूं मैं,

4. Adjustments

What kind of planning? The kind that is convenient, which lightens your workload and allows you to enjoy life without the burden of work.

Let me start with housework. There are constant worries about what to cook, what to pack in tiffins, and what to prepare for dinner, whether you are a housewife or a working woman. There is a simple solution. First, make a list of dishes that each family member likes. From breakfast to dinner, include a variety of nutritious meals as well as innovative dishes. Plan a special dinner once or twice a month. From this list, identify common dishes that everyone enjoys. Create a weekly timetable from Sunday to Monday, write it down, and display it in your kitchen. This habit of making lists, which I developed in childhood, now helps me plan all my tasks, making my work seem easy and simple. You will save an hour each day, as the constant question of "what to cook?" will be resolved.

Do you work or run a small business from home? If you have a fixed job, divide your daily tasks around your work hours. If you wake up at 6 am, try waking up 15 minutes earlier. These extra 15 minutes will make your entire day easier. If you work from home, set specific working hours and plan the remaining time for family and housework.

Those facing obstacles from family or husband need to make a special effort. Prepare a detailed checklist, including household expenses, travel costs, and savings. Explain that increased income will reduce restrictions on spending and increase savings. By calculating and explaining this calmly, you will surely succeed. The list in the kitchen will help you remember everything, from buying vegetables to grocery shopping. Gradually, everyone's favourite dishes will be included in the list.

Gaining permission to work outside will boost your confidence. Although many women today are independent, there are still families where women are expected to stay home. This planning will be very useful for working women. Just two days ago, I met a women's association where 99% of the women said they had no time for themselves. So, plan to make time. You often compromise on everything. I recently heard someone say, "If an elder or even a child is sick, do men take leave? No. Why? Because we always have to take leave."

Make a timetable that fits your housework and working hours so that you have time for yourself. Importantly, this does not mean living like a robot. Keep a list of everything, from extra clothes to snacks, medicines, and water for a picnic. People who know me often call and ask for my lists.

Previously, I kept a small diary and pen. Now, with notepads on phones, you can easily prepare lists for any trip, be it a few days or a week. Sometimes, we even carry groceries with us. Keep a list of ingredients needed for dishes like kanda poha. This way, you'll be relaxed and ready for surprise trips or outings without any worry.

I prepare my things 20-25 days in advance. My mum often laughs at me, asking why I prepare clothes so early. I always reply that as a businesswoman, I need to be ready for any sudden meetings or work. I keep a checklist in my purse, ensuring I don't forget anything. Many women wait until the last minute, but having a checklist keeps everything organised.

Some women inform the milkman and greengrocer just a day before leaving. I suggest keeping a list for closing the house too. Note down what needs to be done and set reminders on your phone. This will save you time and help you relax. You will appreciate how much this list helps.

If your child has exams, allocate subjects and study times for him. List your daily routine to find time for yourself. Avoid watching TV serials like "Anupama." It's a fictional story, and discussing it wastes precious time. Instead, use your intelligence and focus on reality.

Prioritise yourself. Spend time doing things you enjoy, whether it's having tea by the window, reading, listening to music, or talking to a friend. I have a close friend with whom I recently spent an evening. Despite working hard, she told me how her 13-year-old son demands dinner as soon as she gets home. I advised her to value herself and teach her son to be independent.

When children turn 11, let them do small tasks themselves. By 13, they should understand that parents also get tired from work. Teaching kindness and independence is crucial for their development.

I am part of the BNI organisation, where I served as president for 8 months. During a training session led by Director Dr. Nidhi Singhvi, she advised that when you make someone a partner in your work, God provides enough for both. This resonated with me.

Earlier, I managed all the work myself, keeping a list for distribution. Now, I delegate tasks to workers, even for household chores. Supporting someone's livelihood brings double blessings in return.

One woman worked hard to support her family. Her daughter, who helped her, got married. She hadn't taught her son to appreciate her efforts. Now, he wastes time instead of helping. Teaching children to value hard work is essential.

Smart work means dividing tasks to find time for yourself. Hire help for household chores if needed. Set specific times for customers if you run a home business. Don't let work disrupt family time.

Be mindful of your needs and keep a list of essentials. Planning and organising tasks will streamline your work and give you direction.

Say no to tasks you cannot do. Enjoy the things you commit to. Our workshop operates from 9:30 am to 6 pm. One evening, a customer arrived at 7:30 pm. I politely informed him that we were closed. It's important to maintain work-life balance.

Effective planning ensures you won't forget anything, even for school meetings or family events. Keep a list of relatives for sudden invitations. Choose clothes that make you happy and prepare them in advance. Proper planning for events prevents any mishaps.

Office celebrations and training programmes also benefit from good planning. Your husband will appreciate your efforts when he doesn't have to remind you of forgotten tasks. My mother taught me to be prepared for emergencies, and planning has made my work easier.

Your family will support your planning efforts, and you will find moments for yourself. It's not about who is in the cradle, but who holds the cord. When Jijabai holds the cord, Shivaji grows strong. No matter the era or location, effective planning leads to success.

Tell me, dear Anupama, you worry so much about yourself. 80% of your problems can be solved.

You like to sit by the window with a cup of tea or have coffee in a cosy spot. You enjoy listening to a nice song, reading something you like, or talking to someone you care about. Do what you love. I have a close friend, and we recently spent a night together. We sat and talked a lot. Around 12:30 am, we made coffee, and her younger son joined us.

We happily reminisced about old times. Then my friend started telling me, "I work so much, and even if I get tired, as soon as I come home, my 13-year-old son says, 'Mum, give me dinner first.'" I explained to her that if she doesn't value herself, no one else will.

I advised her to explain to him, "Mum has come from work and is tired. You bring me water." He has been watching TV in the air conditioning at home. Teach your child to be independent, not helpless.

When a child turns 11, let him do small tasks himself. If he is over 13, explain gradually. Just as he gets tired from playing, we also get tired from working. If you don't teach him, he won't learn. You are teaching him kindness not just for you but for every human being.

I joined a BNI organisation, where I served as president for 8 months. During our LT training, which lasted about two hours, Director Dr. Nidhi Singhvi gave excellent advice. She said, "When you make someone a partner (worker) in your work, God provides more than enough to feed them." I found this very inspiring.

Earlier, if I was going away for a week, I used to share all the work and keep a list with me. Now, I distribute the work to others. This advice is for women who work from home but hesitate to delegate housework or cooking tasks. They think, "What will be left for me to do?" This is the wrong mindset. When you support the livelihood of those you hire, the Lord gives you double in return. I have experienced this myself.

One woman worked hard to support her family. Her daughter was a great help but got married and moved to her in-laws'. The woman's son, expected to support her, was never taught the value of hard work. He spends all his time roaming around. Why? Because we only know how to work tirelessly without smart planning.

Smart work doesn't cost much. Divide tasks to find time for yourself. Find a work partner or domestic help if you work outside the home. Many women complain that they can't complete all the work on a single Sunday off. The solution is to divide the work.

"Lakshman Rekha" wasn't drawn to dictate that house cleaning should be done only during Diwali. Set a specific time at your convenience to clean the house regularly. Don't let garbage accumulate. Daily work will become easier.

Just as our children organise their schoolbooks according to the timetable, keep a list of tasks for work. Check the list regularly to ensure nothing is forgotten. This will save time in the long run.

Nowadays, people want to hang out with friends after watching reels on social media. If you don't enjoy it, these outings can feel like a punishment. Instead, spend time with someone you truly like. There is no age limit for this.

Research shows that groups of women over 40 have started to travel more. They realise that the first 20 years were spent in education and the next 20 in marriage and raising children. When will they live for themselves?

It's not too late. You can save time by planning each task. Even when I didn't have any system or workers five years ago, I lived this way. Now, despite having work, I am free.

I was surprised when I read the book "One Minute Manager" because I have been organising work since childhood, assigning each task according to a list. Our papad industry has completed 26 years. My mum worked there for 10 years, and we have been helping her since childhood. I have been in charge for 16 years. Even in my presence, I distribute the work list, and in my absence, the list is given to the workers in writing. Whether I am out for a week or ten days, there is no need to worry or call. I have a group of 15-16 women who travel with me, and they all know this system.

Make your calendar your reminder friend.

Write notes in the calendar by date, whether it's a work note or a wedding you need to attend. Give your entire staff a list of what extra work they can do in your absence.

Make a list of the things you need, whether it's food, grain, water at home or in your factory, workshop, or office. This list should be checked every 15 days. Even the smallest items, like a pin, should be included. This will help you avoid unnecessary mental stress.

Do you work from home? Very nice. Whether you are selling clothes, doing nail art, or running a beauty parlour, set specific times for these activities. Your customers will adjust to your schedule. Dinner time at home and someone arrives for eyebrow threading, or to view clothes during your children's homework time? We feel compelled to attend to them because it is our daily bread. But if you want your business to be sustainable, you must plan.

Be mindful of your own small needs, like using a pad, a cream, or powder. Make a list, check it, and stay calm. You can handle the planning yourself. Just list your tasks, allocate time for each, and follow through. This will ensure your work proceeds smoothly.

Honestly say no to what you can't do. Only then will you enjoy doing the other tasks.

Our workshop is also close to home. We have set specific working hours, from 9:30 am to 6:00 pm. One day, a customer arrived at 7:30 pm. I politely informed him, "Sir, the office is closed. Today I will make an exception, but next time please collect your orders by 6:00 pm."

He replied wisely, "Sister, you should be grateful for God's grace that you are still receiving an income." I agreed, acknowledging that without divine grace, we are nothing. However, God also instructs us to eat at mealtimes and spend time with our families.

I considered the idea of having someone work from 6:00 pm to 10:00 pm, but realised that this time is meant for home and family.

Effective planning will teach you a lot. If I keep the shop open from 6:00 pm to 10:00 pm, late customers might start coming regularly. Be honest about your work, and everything will naturally fall into place.

If there is a meeting at the school, plan for it in your diary. You need to organise meetings throughout the year.

This applies to both housewives and working women. Small and big events occur frequently at home. Participate in the planning. Understand the details of small and big rituals and customs, and keep a list of these too.

Also, maintain a separate list of your 50 closest relatives, so you don't forget anyone in case of an unexpected event.

Wearing a nice gown or saree is a must. But choose clothes that make you happy. Prepare according to your convenience, not to impress others.

Keep a list for each event and use it as a checklist. This way, you can ensure that no relative's needs are overlooked.

There are many celebrations in the office as well. Training programmes are conducted regularly. Planning will help you manage these tasks smoothly.

Your husband will greatly appreciate your efforts, as you won't need to call him for help or have him constantly reminding you about forgotten tasks.

My mother taught me to be prepared for any situation. Planning for every task makes unexpected or urgent work much easier to handle.

Your family will support your planning efforts, and the biggest advantage is that you will find moments to live for yourself. Find time for yourself.

It is not important who is in the cradle, but whose hands hold the cord of the cradle. When that cord is in the hands of Jijabai, then Shivaji grows. No matter the era, the geography, or the people.

5. Simplicity

You will become very relaxed yourself. We know that only women can handle everything at home and in the office. Then, work will become very easy without burdening you, and you will develop a simpler nature. Whenever a new opportunity comes before you, you will start accepting it because everything will become easier for you.

You will have planned for each task, so you will find everything very easily. Be it at home or the office, you will be able to organise your belongings in an orderly manner. The checklist you have prepared will ensure that items are organised as planned.

It is mostly women who take the lead in tidying up and decorating every home. So, when there is an office, a large factory, or a small-scale industry, look carefully. Where women are employed, things are arranged beautifully. When their boss (owner) wants anything from them, they can provide it quickly. If you have a planned arrangement at home, you can easily answer calls from home during work hours and find things while sitting.

Now, look at places or factories where only men work. Often, they are in a messy condition. Therefore, women create a home-like environment wherever they work.

It is said that "cleanliness reigns supreme." In a house that is chaotic, dirty, or cluttered, one cannot prosper. God likes a tidy and clean house as much as a clean mind. So, you must plan to complete every task easily, which also helps you decide your budget. You may have noticed that when you dress up and look in the mirror, you feel beautiful. A new energy fills your body, and everything looks beautiful.

Similarly, completing each task easily brings joy and infuses you with new energy. Determine what percentage you should save for travel, shopping, and unexpected expenses. If you have planned all this on paper (in a diary), you will be able to adjust with time.

A report from our society stated that a woman who runs a business does so for her family. When the family has unexpected expenses, the cash saved in the "closet" comes in handy. If you plan this way, it makes everything easier.

If you determine the balance sheet of all income and decide the budget for the whole year in advance, saving money becomes easier. Wealth will follow if you distribute it in a planned way. Your personal expenses, travel expenses, or kitty party expenses will not become a burden. If you are a business owner, you are solely responsible for the business. Whether it is a small-scale business or a large family business, confusions are always there. If the husband supports the family, it causes problems, and if the family supports the husband, he gets confused. What can we do in such a situation?

On one side is our business, where our name is attached, from which we get our daily bread, and many people (workers) are associated with us. In such a situation, planning helps get things done easily. Planning involves sharing the work. If the family objects to your plans, sit down and talk to them. Explain the importance and benefits of your work. If you communicate, it will be easier. If you get confused, it will only worsen.

Whether you do business, work a job, or are independent, first be a responsible woman. Understand your responsibilities before speaking because you have a responsibility to your family and to your office or factory. One working woman asked me, "Sister, I adjust everything, yet everyone fights with me, and my relationships deteriorate." I asked her, "Is work or relationship more important to you?" She said, "My livelihood comes first. Who will provide for me without it?" I said, "If you want to run your business, relationships are important. Think about how responsible you are for yourself, and you won't fight with anyone." It has been three years since that conversation, and everything has become easier for her.

Perhaps reading this will give you an idea of how, with the help of a pen and book, life can be easier for everyone. Yes, I agree, but those who try are sure to win. When you focus on how you are for everyone, not just how you are for yourself, you will find the way.

About ten years ago, a woman came to meet me. She was troubled. God had given her lovely sons, but her husband was a bit addicted to alcohol, though religious. Her family was moderate but spent money on superstitious practices.

I accept that there is positive and negative energy on earth, and I have experienced both. So, I respect everyone's faith.

That woman is good-natured and very devoted, but the whole family believes in superstitions, making the situation difficult. She talked to me, saying, "We pray, we chant, but our days don't improve." So I asked, "Are you chanting?" She replied, "100 malas for this, 1008 for that..." I said to her, "If you have come to me with faith, I will tell you one thing: God is not many, but one. Take shelter in one. Choose one deity. Leave all these superstitions. All gods are ours. Just hold a Panth (Guru) with faith and stay away from such superstitions." Today, her life is very easy. Everything is simple; we make it hard.

God has placed thorns on every road. Whether you lift them to the side, change the road, or cross the road by stepping on the thorns is up to you. Nothing is easy in this world! You have to make it easy. Compromises over time teach you adjustment, and your planning makes it easier for you.

Many women were sitting and gossiping. I will not name any TV show, but there was one being discussed the most. Mostly, the women involved were employed. I had to ask, "Aunty, what's in this serial? If you're tired, take some sleep. Why waste your time on it? Tell me, does it refresh your mind? Or does it deteriorate your brain and increase quarrels in the family?"

In these serials, one husband has two or three affairs. People leave their spouses and marry two or three others. A husband and wife are doing well until a villain enters between them. Is all this really for your entertainment? It doesn't matter if it is. But when a woman sees all this and falls into her fantasy world, even the good things about her family will start to feel bad to her. Then her wants and needs start to increase, and when these are not fulfilled, both her mind and brain become confused. This effect also affects working women, whether they have an office job or a business. Watch it, no one says no, but just for entertainment, not to find a way to make yourself miserable by comparing it to your real world.

Let's think that such an effect does not impact our psyche. The workload and responsibilities are often so puzzling in our real life that we attach this imaginary world to it. All work will be easy for working women if they organise it as planned. Whether you are managing ₹10 lakhs or ₹10 crores, a checklist of tasks, their planned arrangement, distribution of work accordingly, and the habit of completing work within the given time will make all your tasks easier.

Many women enjoy having tea, finding peace in it. There's nothing wrong with it; it relaxes you, and you must enjoy it. There are some complaints like, "Today I left my tea." That is why we forget ourselves amidst all these responsibilities.

There is only one life you have. You are also a human being. Be alert, be active. Be it a family problem or any confusion in business, brainstorm on it in a way that makes sense to you. If you can't, consult someone. Often, your confusion is small. You ask for advice, whether the other person understands it or not, and then it gets messy.

Think for yourself (whether you are working or a housewife). Make your favourite things, eat them. Watch your favourite movie, listen to your favourite song, and play with the little kids instead of feeling sad when something worries you or someone scolds you. I often eat ice cream with the children on my street. I don't know why, but I have a lot of fun doing it. Visit a place or temple of your choice, not every day, but on weekends.

No one in the house may want to eat ice cream, but if you crave it, you earn, so order it or go and eat it. Life isn't fun when everything is straightforward; some ups and downs are necessary. Only then do we understand the difference between happiness and sadness.

I am living because I am writing. One day my husband fell ill. He began to worry that he might have a serious illness. To support him, I also ate the same simple food—khichdi, raab, etc.—for 10-15 days. I felt he was more upset by overthinking than by the disease. We sat and explained that he should not worry. I assured him that in case of anything, I would take him directly to Mumbai (to Kokilaben Ambani Hospital). He asked, "Do you think so for me?" I said, "No, I am ready for every situation. I'm not a woman who cries over her husband, wondering what will happen next." And he was relieved, knowing his wife would not let anything happen to him.

The only thing you earn is to be a bit alert. Don't be like a donkey, doing housework in the morning and then attending to your kids and husband. No, love your work, and work will love you back. Many times you have seen incidents in the news or on mobile where women are brutally tortured. You cannot change everything, but if you change yourself, everything will change automatically. Many women can be softer than women and more rigid than men. She is not emotionless, but her situation prepares her.

Time, circumstance, compromise, and planning. You can overcome all this when you follow it yourself and make it your culture. After this, we will also know how to maintain culture with success.

दुनिया मे कहीं भी हमारा नाम नहीं है,
इसलिए ही तो इस दुनिया का नाम है।

6. Success

What is success? Is it what people have decided for you, or what you have accepted yourself as being successful? We often hear, "I don't have time. I had to attend this programme. I tried hard to complete the work, but could not finish in time." Indeed, those who say they don't have time are often free. If others are working, let them work. I have a lot of work; I am also a businesswoman. But when I genuinely want to go somewhere, I arrange and complete my work or plan something. This is possible only when you truly want to go. All work will be managed, but worship of God will be left out. Do what is left first, then nothing is left undone. Here, I present a very short experience of 20-25 women working in almost different fields.

First of all, my staff is only women. There are about 15 of them. I asked them, "Have you been making papad for 25 years? Do you feel burdened? Do you feel any load that everyone goes to weddings, and you don't get to go or get leave? How nice it must be for everyone to rest while you work all day."

Someone said, "When we come here, we forget all the worries and sorrows of home."

Someone else said, "Since we joined the papad-making, we have been on many pilgrimages. We had plans to go to Bardoli Surat (city)."

Another mentioned, "All the kids studied and got good jobs. We didn't have to go into debt to teach them."

Someone noted, "All the furniture of the house is made by making papad."

Another added, "Our daughters learn well from here and lead a good life at their in-laws'."

Finally, someone said, "Money has never been such a problem that we have to cry."

Here is the story of my papad family. And now, I asked the women working in another place, "Sister, you are independent, you can use money as you wish. How do you feel?" She replied, "Sister, the strife in my house has stopped. People do help, but how long will it last? Such awareness came, and today I can even go out with my own money."

Someone said, "With my husband's money, we save for loan instalments and monthly expenses. With my earnings, household expenses like milk and vegetables are managed."

Another said, "We are from a joint family. We fully support the family. Due to our income support, we were able to afford a car today."

This is also called success, when your work makes you happy.

Chandrayaan-3 was launched on 14 July 2023 and successfully landed on 23 August 2023. The ISRO team included women (attired in sarees) throughout the programme. There are many examples for intelligent people who try to belittle women with sayings like "Baira ni Buddhi Pag ni Pani Ma" (meaning women's intelligence is in the heel of their legs). Today's women succeed alongside men. In 2013-14, when I used to organise small and big programmes in the village street, the whole street was filled with immense joy. It was a lot of fun. Not only the little kids or the youth but the street elders also enjoyed a lot, blessing me greatly. This continued for all festivals and events. Everyone, big and small, started calling me by a nickname. I also wrote in my bio (Mind Reading) that I am happiest when everyone is happy with me. Gradually, we managed the village programme for a street of 177 people. Everything was going well.

In such a situation, the great ideas of two or three intelligent men and women "a woman does business" made this poison fit into the mentality of everyone. The poison of jealousy crossed such a limit that in 2019, this poison destroyed all the people who lived happily. Not everyone was happy to see each other's faces. Elder brothers provoked the young friends to create such commotion that the entire lake of love was stained with mud puddles.

My anguish of mind made me so strong that I will be honest in my work and do more than I have worked hard, but I will remove the belief that a woman does business. Do you understand women? And in which generation do you live? I got inspiration from the life of the late Sushma Swaraj, who was the External Affairs Minister. There was no mistake in her administration. We are women, so some people want to sideline us. Why should we be sidelined? No. I was so angry at that time that "all these TV serials have conspiracies. Can it be done among our people? But when jealousy becomes unbearable, it releases venom more poisonous than a cobra.

I had a friend who has passed away. She gave me good advice to calm me down. "Often it happens that we fall in love with shoes, and the crown watches our way," were her last words for me, and indeed today, it has been six years. I am in a place where people listen to me. I get invited to factories or other industries to teach something to their workers.

The reason for telling this story is that in any situation, if you are right and stand firm, victory is yours.

Not even the Himalayas can shake strong-minded women. Be powerful for yourself, not to compare with men.

The list of successful women in this modern era is extensive. Astronauts Kalpana Chawla and Sunita Williams, athlete P. T. Usha, the first woman President Pratibha Patil, the first woman Prime Minister Indira Gandhi, and India's first woman photojournalist, named the "First Lady of the Lens" by Google, from a Parsi family in Navsari. Nowadays, reels (social media) are seen by many. Every two days, a woman (daughter) achieves something.

Yet many societies are still blindfolded. "No, don't get involved in women's talk." Now that you are doing so much work, just take care of the house. Many such comments are heard around us. Just be educated for what you work for. Make good use of your time. 80% of the girls enjoy watching and making reels.

We have written further that you are working. You are a responsible woman, whether working for home or your office. You've planned, and your work just got easier. Then, whether it is the planning we do or the planning that succeeds, you preserve the culture. There is a slogan in English:

"Culture makes people understand each other better."

Culture inspires us to learn to enjoy each other more. Whether you have a business or are working somewhere, many places have training programmes. We learn something new in the new system. We keep our culture together. A beautiful prayer is offered after all the employees are present. During the prayer, work is on halt for five minutes. Visitors and office staff address each other with Jai Mataji. If 90% of our staff is women, it is natural that they have left home after working. So, when they start the work by praying, new energy is imparted.

You have a small office with a staff of 4-5, and if they are female, ask for their wishes at least once a year. Plan a one-day trip somewhere or have a nice dinner with them. A family atmosphere will be maintained at your place of business as well.

There are many training programmes in today's modern times. We have been organising many of these picnic trips for over 15 years. When I participated in a training programme and was taught this, I came to know that this is called a business strategy, which we do.

You do the job, develop your own culture. Always smile. Learn to bow and greet everyone. Do the work of your colleagues and friends; they will do yours in return.

I see many women entering the office with a twelve o'clock expression. I had to visit a doctor there 2-3 times recently. Their receptionist looked at us with both legs crossed, a pen in her mouth, and headphones (Bluetooth) in her ears. I asked, "Is the doctor available?" "Yes," she replied. Neither a smile on her face nor a polite word. You have to speak up. If you work in this way, the patient will run away.

Give 100% in whatever you do. God will double it, but don't expect it. Let us be a priority in our lives. Work on yourself so much that you can see yourself succeeding. Whether you have planned for your business, home, or work, you must be ready to go with it first. Only then will it bring you success easily.

Keep changing your rules and work plans from time to time. The deeper you delve into your work, the more alert you become. Successful people don't do anything different. They make the way of working different.

In these 21 years of business, I never thought about when I would be successful. My close relatives and friends often tell me, "We want to learn to hold the mic like you. I want to do the same as you."

God's blessings are on me. I never thought I would act or dress like this. My choice is very simple. My friends tease me by calling me 'grandma/elderly,' but I am happy with it.

When I attend our business group meetings wearing a suit (blazer) and shoes, someone meets me and asks, "What business are you doing? Have you started any new business?" I say that I am presenting only my papad. "What else is there to sell?" they ask.

"Let's open a shop there," someone suggests. Even hearing such things, something comes to mind for them, seeing us like this. But when you know that you are successful, such questions will not irritate you. Be proud of yourself.

To be successful, keep up with the news and systematically follow your culture. I too rely on pen and paper to balance society, customs, and business. I perform my duties very well. Our business extends from home to abroad. Naturally, my phone rings every two minutes. We make adjustments so that even when I go out of state, our customer's calls are answered on time. Ours is not a very big, but a nice home business, which we have tried to level well and will continue to do so, ensuring timely responses and service to the customer. You will be successful in your work, and naturally, your spouse will associate you with trust in his work.

You are a working woman. Always keep a record of your financial transactions. Discuss it with your husband or trusted family members and give them a copy of your records.

> हम चाहे वहां उजाला को,
> आना ही पड़ता है,
> क्योंकि रोशनी हमारे ही,
> हाथोंकी लकीर जो है।

7. Freedom

A woman loves kajal, bindi, jewellery, new clothes, but above all these things, she loves freedom and her dreams...

What is freedom? If you are free from your own thoughts first, you will be free to express your opinion everywhere. And when you do everything with a free mind, you will do it with new energy. A positive attitude will emerge in you.

Thoughts and stereotypes have bound you. There is nothing wrong with being freed from the shackles of fear and dread.

Maybe whoever is reading this book right now, you may not be thinking like me or even living like me, but I am saying this based on your surroundings and behaviour. A woman was behind me in a departmental store, D-Mart. We had our bags locked and checked inside. She was trying to remember something. I had a list, so I didn't have to brainstorm too much, but I was reading the expiry dates, so I had to listen to them. I heard the staff there saying, "Sister, the sale is over?" talking about the discount. The staff said, "No... no... a few things are finished. I have been shouting for days, but he was not free to bring me here." I asked, "Which village are you from?" She said, "I am from a nearby village." It takes 10 minutes in a rickshaw. A rickshaw will come to your village in the same way as society on a single call. Yes, you are right, but a well-known rickshaw driver is good. I said, "Sister, you have to make him well-known so that the work is done on time." It's a small matter, but it takes time.

Even in the Women's Day programme, I uttered this sentence two to three times: a woman is also the enemy of a woman and a woman is also the friend of a woman. No situation compels them to make such enemies. All this is revealed by their conservative mentality. Be alert for a while, then see. Now social media is filled with women's sarcasm, and 80% of the jokes are women's comments. There are some songs in Gujarati that demean women in general. I have no objection to that as an art form, but there should be some awareness. It is for every woman. It's not just about working women. When you work in an office or any place, you must be free to speak. In every factory or office, women mostly work. A nice bathroom for them, a pad for their periods—all these things should be arranged so that she can freely say without hesitation that our factory or office has arranged things so we can talk about periods openly and be free from stereotypes. Educate yourself and your family about this. As for religion, you work in a good position or own a factory, yet you leave religion and stick to superstition. We can see how many scandals are exposed on social media today, and women are more involved than men. All such heretics are to be avoided.

Today, women are respected everywhere, but no one wants it to go further. This is my own experience. They have to move with a lot of limitations. The door to freedom will open for you when you move away from the debate, and this debate comes from our self-made laws. I will give you a small example.

A lady died around 3.30 pm. She was already sick. She was about 72 years old. At 7.30 pm, it was decided to take her for cremation. I was involved in all the preparations. It is natural that I cannot change the tradition that has been going on for years, and there is no opposition to it. As she was being taken out of the house, one sister said, "Hey, we forgot to put an axe... now as if something big has happened." She told another one, "You had to remember." Another sister said, "The family should be aware." And I questioned them, "Why do we put an axe?" The previous sister said, "Everyone does, but I don't know why. We also put it with my father-in-law." If you don't know the facts behind it, why are you doing such a thing?

It may be that in earlier times, due to not being able to get enough wood, they used to carry an axe, or if it fell short of burning, the wood was cut. All quiet. We have to make our thoughts independent of such beliefs. For any practice to start, there must be some firm reason. We are responsible for connecting it with religiosity and custom. Beliefs such as not carrying khichdi or dhokla on a journey. We carry khichdi on every trip. All journeys are successful. It happens as you think, because you start to feel like, "This guy brought khichdi and the incident happened."

It means that we are wasting our minds and precious time in this life by connecting everything with superstition instead of living. Then from where we had to get free time apart from housework.

A friend of mine always says whenever she meets me, "I want to be like you." It doesn't happen as you live by accepting reality.

I too have lived through those times and places. We had a professional training programme ongoing, and I participated in it. On one of the training days, we were given the task of making a card for our spouse with a nice message for their birthday. We were given about 20 minutes. I made cute little heart shapes, applied the red colour (my husband's favourite), and created a zigzag design. I made a nice card and wrote a message in it, something like this: "You have given me the freedom that a daughter is trusted to have in her father's house. I will never forget nor abuse it." Almost four to five years have passed since this training programme, and my husband has kept the card well. Just like this, you will also get freedom. Only then can you go out to work.

I also organised a programme (of about 21 women) every month to make all the women aware and attentive to their work, in which training was arranged from saving money to learning recipes. These programmes have been very successful. Women associated with them get a lot of pleasure. They feel that they are alive. Without understanding what the programme was, two or three smart women from outside insisted on stopping it, and someone close to me said, "Are you going to make these people Queen of Jhansi? They are good in their house." How much negativity is there that they can't afford this much freedom. I am not talking about years ago, just two or three years ago.

Why do you want to walk down the street after work? There is no question about it. There is someone to ask you too. If you come from work and go to cheer up your mind, then it is good/Ramlila, and if we come from work and settle the household chores again, if we go out even for ten minutes, then it is considered drama? Where can she go? As and when she finishes her housework, her kids' tuition work is there. Once a month she goes to cheer her mind, so what is wrong with that?

Many programmes in our society do garba, dance, and bhajan. In all these, the communities of our society gather and present their art in one place. Then you get to meet many women. It is like dancing for a few moments out of a cage. From the time they start their practice until the programme presentation is over, they all get together for about a month, then they all go back to work in their nests. We also organise picnics and tours. Then we have fun with knowledge throughout the journey. At the end of the journey, after all the houses gather together, some of the sisters write a message and send it. "Thank you very much. I had so much fun today after a long time." It seems to me that God has created every life on earth. Everyone has been given the art of living. But only in human beings is a man allowed to do what he wants, while a woman cannot.

For the last two years, the caravan of 40+women has burst out. I have also written before that Facebook and Instagram are full of their videos. This is a very good thing. Nothing is wrong with it. Keep travelling and exploring. Our Gujarati sayings are also strong, "Fare te charre, bandhyo bhukhe mare," which means keep moving and travelling. How? By planning. So you won't have trouble. Keep savings for travel as well. If you earn this much, save this much and take this amount for travel, and it might vary, but there will be no significant difference.

Along with freedom of thought, the support of your family, especially your partner, is also very important.

Let me talk about two different working women. One who does not get the support of her husband with the freedom to work, then how suffocated one feels.

I have met her (the woman) probably twice. One meeting was short. The second time, she came to drop me off at my village. During that time, she told me many incidents of her life. When there is a book only for women, why should it be left? There is a middle-class family, a family of three brothers. All living in a small village, in a small house, she decided to live in a nearby town to get a job and teach her kids. She kept working in different places. She managed her house well. Gradually, her skills led to seminars in colleges, training children in all tasks. During all these lifetimes, her son was very intelligent, but he died in a bus accident. During this period, her husband quarrelled every day, drank alcohol, wanted to spend money, and started to annoy her too much. This lady endured everything. After that, her husband overstepped his bounds and raised his hand against her. This went on for some time. A mother's son dies, and it is as if the food before her mouth goes away. And even though she was running the house herself, she received beatings and insults from her husband as a bonus. We can't even imagine what her pain must have been during this time. Finally, the lady broke her silence and kicked him out of the house. And today, every year on her son's death anniversary, she conducts programmes to train students on how to give first aid during an accident at different places, as her son died due to a lack of first aid at the scene. What that woman does at present, we will see in existence.

She will own her existence as she decides to live her life on her own.

*****

Two different women to talk about. I have met these women many times. At first glance, they seem capable of everything. Neither the feeling of sorrow is ever seen on their faces nor do they appear sad. There is always a smile on their faces and a sweet smile at that. When you see them, your own sorrows seem to fade away.

I meet them at programmes in many places. They hold good positions (designations). Many men work under them for all jobs, from car drivers to other roles. I know this because whenever they attend an event, they arrive alone in their cars, whether it is a social programme or a business-oriented one.

What mental anguish might they be enduring? When someone asks these ladies, "Your husband did not appear?" they always avoid answering with a laugh. Once, I delved deeper into the matter. I came to know that he is fine in every way but may have come as the chief guest in this programme. The day has been good. There is no problem throughout the day. But the brainstorming starts ten minutes before reaching home in the evening. "How will my husband feel today? Will he be happy? Will he be upset with me?" The horses of thoughts run very fast before entering the house. It may have happened to her many times that the praises she heard from people all day have drifted into her damp pillow at night. There is hardly anyone who does not have such a chain obstructing them. That woman will not run away. Just don't tie her down. If you tie her down, she will get stuck, and if she is released from there, she will not even be seen. We must free ourselves from the shackles of the mind. Be independent with your staff and colleagues. Let's provide an environment where women who come to our office or factory can smile. Her mind should not be burdened with work.

The one who comes to work smiling and keeps smiling through her work. Many sisters say that when we go to work, we forget all our sorrows. Love your work, and it will love you back. When you simplify all your tasks, you will become independent from everything. Having a set budget will hold you accountable and help others when you're stuck. Helping someone with your money will bring a different joy to your face, and it will make you feel twice the joy than wearing jewellery worth crores of rupees.

Not much, but learn to spend 5% of your earnings, if not 5%, then 2%, for someone in need. You will surely be doing God's work. Today's blind show-off kills humanity too. And it is only a woman who will distribute to everyone in the house what she gets from the house.

Well-known Dr Sudha Murthy, who has written eight novels, is the first woman to work for India's largest auto engineering and locomotive company, and she is also a social activist. I remember two things she said, which I am writing about. When you are married, you have to fight, and if there is no fighting between husband and wife, then you are not husband and wife. One has to keep quiet, and one keeps talking. None are perfect. Everyone has ups and downs in life. Accept it. She has given a message to the youth of today's generation to help their wives in the kitchen. Every man says that my wife doesn't cook like my mother, but Sudha Murthy ma'am has specifically told them that mother was not working, and if your wife works, help her with housework. She has said that she has accepted ups and downs in her life too. That is why today she is on the list of successful women. Her daughter is married to Rishi Sunak, Prime Minister of London. I am an ordinary woman sharing my experiences, but when Sudha Murthy ma'am herself says, one realises that a person is shaped by experience and can also educate and understand others from their experiences. When she is successful, she is free to speak her mind. To those who consider women inferior, I specifically tell them that the car in your wish list 'Mahindra Thar' was designed by 49-year-old mechanical engineer Ramkripa Ananthan, who is a woman.

Freedom is not just about having wings to fly. The sparrow comes to its nest in the evening.

When I write about freedom, I remember an experience that happened to me. It was around 2019, and an elder, unsure if there would be any problem with my progress or if I would be a hindrance to his work, told me, "Shall I say something about the Ramayana?" I said, "Yes."

Uncle started talking, "Divya, if Kaikeyi had not gone to war with King Dasharatha, then the Ramayana would not have happened." I remembered. Then after a while, I replied, "Uncle, if the Queen of Jhansi had not taken up the sword to fight the British and driven them away, then Jhansi would not have been freed." What he meant to imply indirectly was that a woman should remain beautiful where she is. That's why I say, be cautious.

लोग पूछते है तुम कौन हो?
आपको पता नहीं ?
मैं विश्वनिर्मात्री हूं।
आप दर्द से मुजे डराते हो?
दर्दको भी मैं जन्म देती हूं।
में दर्दकी भी माँ हूं।
मुजे दर्द क्या डरायेगा?
अब पता चला में कौन हूं?
में नारी हूं।

8. Women – Existence

It is said that when writing about a woman, only a woman can do it well. That may be true, but Kumarilbhai has written something very profound: "The whole existence must have given their everything, then nature must have taken its final step and then it created woman."

It is written in Hindi, but if you read it carefully, you can see that he encapsulated our essence in four lines.

The biggest battle every woman faces is the battle for her own existence. Today, in big companies, politics, as doctors, lawyers, teachers, scientists, chefs—everywhere—women are being recognised for their skills. On the opposite side, the words 'intelligence in foot' are still used for women. It is said that in big institutions it should now be mandatory to have one or more women. Compliance with the order will be certain. Two women will be given their positions, but only to appear on paper.

There are many organisations where women are only in name. They are not consulted, and anything they say is dismissed because they are women. Ninety-nine per cent of decisions are only signed off by them after they are taken. Many times, they do not even know they are members. It is not known which member holds which role. And if a plan is mistakenly given to them, it passes several checkpoints to decide whether to implement it, and even if implemented, it is changed.

In one's programme, a high-ranking woman from outside, like a police commissioner or a collector, will be called to honour the women. Talking to the women of their own society or organisation is a distant thought—they are not supported even behind their backs. If the principal of a school is a woman, the trustees and the management committee do not allow her to make any decisions and even reverse the decisions she makes. We see many such examples.

Amitabh Bachchan ji sang a song: "Tu chal, tu kis liye hatash hai, tu chal tere wajud ki samay ko bhi talash hai." Very true. If you get time, it is worth listening to and pondering over these words.

"To find oneself, one has to meet oneself." If you make a habit of talking to yourself for half a minute every day, you will miss half an hour to meet yourself.

I often comment while holding the mic at a programme that the cat's stomach can't digest the pudding and the woman's stomach can't digest the talk. It is not like that. This is just a saying. If women want to speak their hearts out, they can't even walk in the house with some slanderers. What is inherent in her endurance can never be found in any man. She only fails to find herself. When a daughter gets married, there is a lot of talk, like will she get a job after marriage? Will they allow her to set up her own business? Two or three family members are doing so-and-so, but they are persuaded to get married. Everything will be fine after marriage, they say, it is not a big deal. Why is it not a big deal? Only her heart knows how hard she worked during her school years, how her parents managed to pay the fees. In many families, if the daughter-in-law earns, she will be seen as a threat and not allowed to work, kept busy with housework. Then her self-esteem is hurt. What is mine? Nothing is mine.

We understand we cannot always say that a woman is right always. It often happens that, having a job at a high post, with a high salary, she does not know how to cook. This is common today. Be competent by all means. If you want to be involved in a job or business, then you have to learn small housework and even basic cooking. You have to prepare yourself for your existence. Otherwise, managing a family and a business, you will lose yourself somewhere. What is yours and what will you take with you when you leave?

Be prepared for the coming disaster. Why not even the death of the head of the house? When a major calamity strikes in your home or business, you should be capable enough that no one else has to make a decision for you or your family. And to be capable, you have to be aware. The blind imitation of the fashion world ends with branded clothes to exotic cuisines. Show-off trends are ongoing. A place to visit or a dish to eat. When are we going to post a story on Snapchat?

There is a problem, don't think about it, don't share it with everyone, don't cry. Instead of holding on to the problem, find ways to get out of it.

Two or three workers are on leave, goods are overstocked, or office workers have not come to the office. Learn to manage these moments too. Try to do their work on that day, you will learn something new. Consider the worker (employee) on leave. You got a chance to update something new. Whatever it is, accept it. Learn to accept. The path to self-realisation will be paved. Accept reality. What reality? Let me explain with a very common example. You know that along with home, there is also business and family to take care of. Naturally, you always have to be in a situation like choosing between a well and a pit. Don't shy away from it, challenge it. Read good books and books related to business. Meet business people frequently. Collect information related to the business you own. You will come closer to your being when you are capable of everything yourself. Make your own principles and stick to them. Keep asking yourself questions, "Who am I?" until you get the answer. "I want to do something. Why do I do anything I do today? Am I really doing it for myself or for others?" Right now there are earnings, life goes well, then what? And where am I in all this? Ask yourself a thousand questions, and surely you will find ways to deal with them.

Who am I? A wife, a mother, an engineer, or a traveller? We often define our identity based on others—whether as a husband's wife, a son's mother, a working woman, or an owner. In fact, I do not truly know who I am. We must seek our own soul's welfare and, therefore, understand ourselves. What is the goal of our life? If we set our goal, are we able to fulfil it?

A woman is never weak. As a mother, she has the ability to sustain the existence of the earth and give life to others. So why can't she find her own existence? Women need to wake up.

Wake up and start giving yourself time. We give birth to a child, and its father's name is written on its back. This has been mentioned in many places now. Why so? Because these social systems have been running for ages, and we continue to uphold them.

I heard a nice story somewhere, and it's funny. A woman manages all the household members. Her cooking is commendable; she takes great care of the children, from massaging the feet of the elders on time to tending to the little things for all the family members. Naturally, everyone praises her. So, we climb up the 'peanut tree'. This woman even talks outside, saying, "These people can't live without me. If I am not there, everything will fall apart. Everything is dark without me." However, after some time, her health deteriorates. Slowly, she thinks, "I should go and see how these people will live without me." She gets admitted to a hospital far away from the village and sends a message that she will have to stay there for a few days. Her health actually worsens, and she returns home after three months. Upon returning, she sees that everyone was managing their own work on time, and everything continued as usual in her absence. It means to say that if my son has to eat, I must cook. Nothing will be right at home without me. While doing all these struggles, accept that everything will be done without everyone and everything will be done without us. No one's life stops.

The strongest woman is the one who becomes a house herself to make someone's house a home.

You run away from your own existence. I will never say that I spent 20 years for kids and so and so for my husband and now I am going to live for myself. What about me? Because I enjoy every moment of my life and will live the remaining moments too.

Very often we hear, "The kids grew up, how much trouble did we have? And now they are grown up, they don't keep us well, don't keep us together." Did the kids tell you, "Mum, you do not eat, you feed us"? If you fulfil your duty, do it with joy. Now, what does its lamentation mean?

There is a nice case. I have a colleague friend. We went shopping about 13 years ago, but the habit of writing makes it memorable. We went to a cake shop and felt like eating pastries. I said to my friend, "Let's sit here in the AC and eat." She said, "No, no, the boy is at home. I will go and eat with him." I asked, "Do you want to eat?" She said, "Who doesn't want to eat? But if I tell the boy, he will say, why didn't I bring it for him?" God's grace is upon us. Let me get it for the boy too. Then she stubbornly started telling me, "No, today we will go home and eat." I asked her a question, "If these same boys grow up, go to college, and have frequent picnic parties with friends, will they treat you the same way?" She said, "No, but what is the use of all that now?" I said, "Then don't be sad that you came home alone like this." After all these years, she remembers me. One day we happened to meet. The boy called her, "Mum, we will be late, we will dine out." They are not even asking to bring something for you? I said, "Our whole life ends in p... p... p... p... p... Husband, son, parent, family, then what?"

Does anyone say no to you, refuse to let you eat what you want, or wear what you like? Who refuses to open your heart and smile? No one is stopping you; you are stopping yourself. Let me tell you about my friend circle. Don't know about others' houses. There is no lunch today. Milk and cereal are enough. Why is it enough? Hey, you have got a chance to make and eat your favourite dish. So, you can sit and relax. What's going on? Do you like rain? Get wet. Do you know if the rain contains your tears as if it were raining on your mind? Like a movie? See if there is a sad moment.

Are you upset? Listen to your favourite music. You may be tired from work; take it easy for 10-15 minutes. Talk to your go to person.

I remembered a very close sister—a mother of a son and a daughter. As I said, they are our world. Without them, we see nothing else. She raised them in great distress. She had a house in a good city, and the society in which they lived was also inhabited by good people. Their situation was slightly better than ours. She provided her children with good education and a nurturing atmosphere. In time, her daughter got married abroad, and her husband passed away. It was just the mother and son in the family. Slowly, the years passed. The woman also went abroad, married her son, and settled him well in the same city. The woman stayed to cook for a doctor's family to support her son's settlement abroad. In case of illness or any other problem, she would bear everything single-handedly for her son and daughter. In time, her son also went abroad with his family, and after everything was settled, the daughter said goodbye to her mother. She spent her whole life behind her children and her family, and what is left of her? Back to the same lonely life? Where there is nothing, everything is zero.

God is not at fault here. And don't blame your karma. Despite your own indifference and being able to earn for yourself, you exclude yourself from all—your very existence. We ourselves are responsible for this.

Our papad-making family is all women. I teach them this: whatever extra they get from here, be it food or anything else, they should use for themselves. They all truly agree with this.

Children are yours, family is yours, responsibility is yours. No one says no, but along with all this, you are your own responsibility; fight for your survival. Don't build your own path to be zero. If you earn, you are capable. If you are a housewife, do save. Be better than pretending that the husband has a good personality. Be competent. Living for yourself is necessary.

I just met a woman at an event this morning. She was speaking to the president of our trust. As I approached, he said, "This sister will definitely help you; her business is going well." So, I started talking as the President moved away. If I talked about work, she said, "First, I need a salary enough to run the house. I want to buy a house and educate my son." Our president said that we would provide a house for her to stay in and that she needed to find a job. She replied, "My job is in Surat." I asked, "Why do you need help then?" She said, "I need both a house and a job, and the salary should be good." I asked, "Are you computer literate?" She said, "No." I asked, "Do you want to get married?" She said, "There are proposals, but I have so many thoughts." I told her, "Sister, don't be mistaken. You need to decide first what to do. You came to this city for job help and are still 40 years old. If the son is adoptable, you should be married. Do you know what to do? How will you raise your son? Our organisation will take responsibility for teaching him until he learns, but you need to make some compromises for yourself. Do you have any relatives living in the house? What do you do then? Or are you registered in the government housing scheme?" We did not understand what to do in this case.

Keep in mind that you cannot abandon your existence in this way.

Jaybhai Vasavada has said well, "If you keep learning, you will live long." If you feel something is missing, find it and complete it, but don't sit back. God has sent you to this earth and also given you the responsibility of home, family, and business. Surely you will find them, and this is only possible when you stop worrying about what the other sister is wearing. To refresh your mind, watch a reel on Instagram, then take a nice cup of tea or coffee or any drink you like and talk to yourself. If you have done something wrong, laugh a little at it and try to correct it. If you have done good work, thank God for giving you the inspiration to do this good work today. Thank you, God. Greetings.

When you understand yourself, you will start appreciating the work of others. I have experienced this. Thank your working family, whether inside your home or in your office or factory, for a job well done. When you are not able to give something, gather everyone together and praise their work. If you have a good customer, give them a small gift for providing good work throughout the year. Have lunch with your office or factory staff. All these are necessary for our existence as women. What you do for yourself is crucial. When you appreciate the people around you in this way, you will find someone who appreciates you, and you will meet your existence when you become a good manager.

My friend, listen only to the voice of your heart, not to the noise of the whole world.

9. Peace

We think there should be peace in each of our homes. In the present time, every one or two people leave, and the third person has to go somewhere to find peace. A famous doctor from Surat, whom I spoke to a few days ago, mentioned that 90% of people are looking for peace of mind. His work involves meditation and Pranic healing, a method that works for the life force of our body, which we cannot see. The biggest and most important reason for unrest, I believe, is that today we live a life of show.

If we turn off our phones for two days, there will be 99% peace, but this will last only for those two days. The peace we seek should stay with us for life, but that is unlikely. However, if we try, we will be successful. "The world stands on hope."

If you are a working woman, peace may become a bit of a tough subject for you. As I have written earlier, think and live for yourself, and for that, you must maintain your health first.

If you are healthy, everything will be completed peacefully behind you. Our family doctor says, even if we have a headache, we must take medicine. If we get sick, everything can go awry. This is a body that suffers; no one denies that. However, for our health to be good, we must choose food that suits our bodies. Perhaps you have to go to work or the office in the morning, and if you don't have enough time, go for a 25-minute walk in the evening. Do not meditate for hours, but chant 'Om' seven times for five minutes. You can even do this while sitting on your bed when you wake up. Avoid eating late at night. If you have to work sitting in a chair all day, reduce the use of elevators. Use the stairs more often to ensure body movement. The first happiness is achieved by yourself. This means staying fit and healthy because a healthy mind can only reside in a healthy body. A healthy body is your priority for leading a peaceful life.

Stop judging others. That's exactly what you do. What if someone had done something differently? If you had asked me once, I would show the truth. Who told you that what you did was right? Deciding for yourself is wrong. Each person is right in their own place. We just need to understand that there is a difference between your situation and theirs. Accept reality. When the son you taught and sent abroad for higher education, understand that there will be a huge difference between his thinking and yours. Yes, you can stop him from doing wrong, but he will make his own life decisions.

A couple of lines used to come up quite often:

The son will marry and be taken away by the daughter-in-law.

The daughter will marry and be taken away by the son-in-law.

In the end, there will be only two of us.

If yes, admit it, it's true. This is why it is natural for us to make arrangements now to be together in the end. If the daughter is married, she will take care of her own house because her duty lies there. And if the son and daughter-in-law live in another city or country, they must have done so to live their own lives. Looking at our past, we too left the village for work. If you get to live with your son and daughter-in-law, consider it the grace of God. Avoid chattering with them over small matters. Listen to them calmly before giving your opinion on anything. We should talk only when necessary. When we are about to become or have become mothers-in-law, it is natural that we have worked and supported this family. When our lives are spent raising kids and running a business with the family, it is painful to live in a son and daughter-in-law narrative. So when the time comes, whatever your son does, consider it good for you. If he is pleased, you are pleased. This is the solution to the peace of our post-retirement days.

First is peace of mind, and second is your control over anger. Whenever you feel angry at the office or home, stop for 10 seconds. Your decision will change drastically. Anger only hurts us. When you have to speak angrily to your employee, you must be firm in your speech, but it should not be bitter. I also used to have a very bad temper when I was not meditating. Things break after anger, the head becomes heavy, and all these losses happen to us. I used to say harsh words to a worker when they made a mistake. In the last 12 years, I don't remember being angry with anyone badly. I have worked on this bad habit of mine. Now, when there is a problem and a worker is responsible, I don't say anything immediately. After half an hour, I gather everyone together, discuss what decision is to be taken, why it happened, and what the solution is. I explain it very gently and calmly. I try my best not to say anything that would annoy or irritate me. Time is strong. We must act according to the individuals and the situation, but if we do it consciously, it makes a difference. There will be no anger. There will be no confusion in the mind. There will be peace.

Be tension-free. God has said that what is going to happen is determined, and what is determined will happen. If you disturb your mind with unnecessary anxiety, you will fall into a state of disrepair. Chant the Gayatri Mantra whenever anxiety starts to rise. Chant the mantra until your mind is free from anxious thoughts. Even if something happens, the chanting of this mantra has the power to turn a sword wound into a needle prick. So, what is going to happen will happen, but we survive a big event and go through some small events, and we get out of that too. It is not necessary to chant the same mantra; you can also remember your own god.

If you are a woman and have an ocean of compassion in your heart, then your heart will not be filled with sorrow and tears. When the mind is troubled, sit near your God and say, "All my worries are at your feet," and smile at them with confidence. Pray to them from the heart. Then see if your anxiety goes away. Chants infuse positive energy into us. When the mind is restless, don't keep things in your mind; let them out. Where should you pour them? Believing in this Kali Yuga is a big question. Pour that also in front of your God. Apologise with folded hands in front of Him if you have made a mistake. Accept your mistake.

Whenever this happens, don't sit in solitude. Solitude makes you Rama and also Ravana. Get out. Take a little walk. Play with the little kids while they play. When the sphere of thoughts is over, calmly find ways to get rid of this difficulty.

I talked to a friend of mine. I asked, "Where did your book reach?" So I sent him a photo of the index. He laughed. I asked why. He said, "Women and peace? It does not set in the mind." Similarly, I have discussed this matter a lot with the doctor from Surat whom I spoke to earlier. He discussed with me that Sri Sri Ravishankarji had narrated a story of Shiva-Parvati.

This is very interesting. Let's see. Lord Shankar is doing his penance in Kailash. God's abode is in Kailash, which is why we call him Kailashvasi. Uma (Parvati) was a virgin/unmarried. She does penance to marry Shivaji, and Uma is called Kanyakumari because she was unmarried. She stands there and does the penance of Shivaji, and Shivaji is pleased with her penance. Shankarji comes south with his band of ghosts to take her away, but the condition is that they must marry before sunrise or not at all. The gods are all worried because if Uma gets married, they will not be able to destroy the devils. If Uma remains unmarried, the gods will be able to destroy the devils. She was blessed with something like that. The gods wanted Uma to remain unmarried to destroy the devils for public welfare. Indra devised a plan. Becoming a chicken, the rooster started making the sound of crowing. So Shivaji's procession stops because it was heard that the sun had risen in the city. At a distance of 25 km from Kanyakumari, there is a place where Shivaji's Var Yatra halted, called Suchitram. That is, the spiritual meaning of being single in human life is that all the desire is to get complete happiness, but when the desire is fulfilled, its happiness is not felt at all. So desire will never reach its goal. Sri Sri Ravishankarji says no one's will has reached its end. Therefore, you cannot reach peace because your desires and needs are not fulfilled. Meditation is the only way for peace of mind, and when you want peace in life, meditate on yourself. Whatever makes you restless, organise your workspace. Change over time what is planned. If you create a principle to follow your plan, stick to it; there must be your culture. Not like the robot configured as the program configures, so it has to be completed.

हम कोई सार्वजनिक तालाब नहीं, जिनका पानी कोई भी आकर पी जाए।
हम कोई ऐसा आवारा पौधा नहीं, जिनको कोई भी आकर सूंघ जाए।
हम कोई ऐसा वैसा फूल नहीं, जिनको कोई भी आकर तोड़ जाए।
हम कोई खेल नहीं इस संसार के, जिन्हें कोई भी आकर के खेल जाए।
हम कोई पवन नहीं, रेगिस्तान के, जिन्हें हर कोई आके उड़ा जाए।
हम कोई ऐसी चिंगारी नहीं, जिन्हें कोई भी आकर जला जाए।
हम ऐसे वैसे खिलौना नहीं, जिनका हाथ कोई भी हाथ मे दिया जाए।
हम खुद ही साम्राज्य है, खुद ही शासन है,
जो जियेंगे खुद के हिसाब से, तय करेंगे खुद के अंदाज से।

Stay away from people with a negative attitude. As I am writing for women, I have mostly focused on women. Has an accident occurred? Be calm. Be the main person to make your decision.

A third important component to peace is trust. I have seen many women, not many, but familiar women too. Once you have a domestic helper or a factory worker, stick to them like lice. They will repeat one thing to them seven times. When I hear this, I tell them that they will forget their work today, and that's what happens. If the worker can read, give it to them in writing. 'Writing will be read' and it will also be remembered that even if you forget, it will happen at times. Trust them, they are there to work for you, so they will do it.

You have taken up a task. Remember God and begin. With faith that you will succeed in this task, be confident. If your son or daughter has gone somewhere to live or on an outing, do not call them 10 times a day instead of working, right? Where did you eat? Who is next to you? Do you like it? Hey sister, you too work in peace and let them roam in peace too. Let them enjoy the place where they have gone. Let them know about it.

Women and peace? Really thought-provoking! You should also go out. Scold your friends in return. Tired of working the whole year? You need to rest a little, refresh your mind. I see all this myself. They will call him from morning. Did dad have tea? What time will you go? Take this much milk today. If you give food (dal rice) to the maid today, if there is a factory, they will ask how many people came? Is the work done? I saw into the camera, all sitting and talking? What time did you leave? What time did the office close? They will ask at home, what did you make? Will dad eat at home or go out to eat? Did grandfather say anything? What did grandmother say?

Oh my mothers, you have gone out for a picnic, come back in peace. I am also involved in business. When going out for fifteen days, I plan for 20 days. Neither do I get any calls from the workplace here nor do I harass them by calling them. They close the office and update me on WhatsApp in the office group.

You left the house. Sitting there, you can't do any work here, then you disturb the work here by calling.

And what happens if there is a minor variation or something goes wrong as per your plan? You have gone thousands of kilometres away, so what are you going to run away from?

I had to go to a programme now. A sister was sitting on the chair next to me. She had the camera running throughout the five-hour programme. I asked why are you doing this? Has anything happened? She said no, no. Nanny is alone at home. Must see as she is with kids. I didn't notice this either, but I was paying attention to every little thing about each sister for this book. I was inquiring, so that I could find something that could do justice to my thoughts and the problems of women. Nothing else, if you believe, the title will come less. And wherever you need peace, you can find peace by your own decision.

In the end, I will say that women are creators. When she does not forget herself to create her life, her existence arises. There is no need to go to the forest to find peace. Find yourself. Peace be with you. You just don't keep it.

I am with you to find the answers to my questions,

May my struggles be resolved by your smile,

May the understanding of your love be my adjustment,

I am with you, may your ease be my success,

I can fly, I can soar, if your freedom lifts me through your wings.

I am not just a woman; your existence gives me peace.

Mother, the only word in the world that does not need any other word in the world. It is in itself the largest dictionary of creation. A mother's lap means the highest peak of peace.

Milton Keynes UK
Ingram Content Group UK Ltd.
UKHW020711251124
451531UK00018B/208